GEOFFREY GRIGSON was born in Pelynt, Cornwall in 1905. He was the editor and founder of *New Verse*; he worked as literary editor of the *Morning Post*, in the BBC Talks Department, and in publishing. He is the author of a great many books. Among them are his *Collected Poems*, published in 1963; *A Skull in Salop* (1967); *Ingestion of Ice Cream* (1969); *Discovery of Bones and Stones* (1971); a volume of criticism, *Poems and Poets* (1968); *Notes from an Odd Country* (1970); and an anthology, *Unrespectable Verse*, published by Allen Lane The Penguin Press (1971).

EDWIN MUIR, who was born in 1887 and died in 1959, is considered to be one of the most distinguished Scottish poets of the twentieth century. His early childhood was spent in the Orkneys but when he was in his early teens his family moved to the slums of Glasgow. The contrast between the two environments haunted Muir and provides the main theme for his *Autobiography* (1954). He managed to give himself a thorough education and published his first volume of poems, *First Poems*, in 1925. After a period living in London he moved with his wife back to Scotland and worked for the British Council in Edinburgh and later in Prague and Rome. Towards the end of his life he was Charles Eliot Norton Professor for a year at Harvard, having spent some years as head of an adult education college near Edinburgh. His other publications include *Scott and Scotland*, *Literature and Society*, a biography of John Knox and one of his finest long poems, *The Labyrinth*.

ADRIAN STOKES was born in 1902. He was brought up in a London that has now largely vanished and was educated at Rugby and Magdalen College, Oxford. Married, with three children, he has lived in Italy, in Cornwall, on the North Downs, and, since 1956, in Hampstead. His publications include *The Quattro Cento* (1932), *Art and Science* (1949), *Painting and the Inner World* (1963) and *Reflections on the Nude* (1967). A selection of his writings has been published in Pelicans as *The Image in Form*.

Penguin Modern Poets

— 23 —

GEOFFREY GRIGSON
EDWIN MUIR
ADRIAN STOKES

—

Guest Editor:
STEPHEN SPENDER

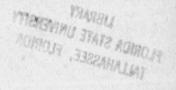

Penguin Books

Penguin Books Ltd, Harmondsworth, Middlesex, England
Penguin Books Inc., 7110 Ambassador Road, Baltimore, Maryland 21207, U.S.A.
Penguin Books Australia Ltd, Ringwood, Victoria, Australia

—

This selection first published 1973

—

The poems by Geoffrey Grigson are copyright
© Geoffrey Grigson, 1963, 1967, 1969, 1971, 1973
The poems by Edwin Muir are copyright © Willa Muir, 1960
The poems by Adrian Stokes are copyright © Adrian Stokes, 1973

Made and printed in Great Britain by
C. Nicholls & Company Ltd
Set in Monotype Garamond

Contents

CONTENTS

EDWIN MUIR

CONTENTS

ADRIAN STOKES

CONTENTS

ACKNOWLEDGEMENTS

For the poems by Geoffrey Grigson from *Collected Poems 1924–1962*, 1963, grateful acknowledgement is made to Phoenix House; for poems from *A Skull in Salop*, 1967, *Ingestion of Ice-Cream*, 1969, and *Discoveries of Bones and Stones*, 1971, grateful acknowledgement is made to Macmillan; and for unpublished poems grateful acknowledgement is made to the author.

For the poems by Edwin Muir from *Collected Poems 1921–58*, 1960, grateful acknowledgement is made to Faber & Faber.

For the poems by Adrian Stokes grateful acknowledgement is made to the author.

GEOFFREY GRIGSON

Under the Cliff

This is when the scarlet lords-and-ladies
Glitter erect in the wet angle of the hedges
And shrivel soon

And again the bland leaves curl and colour,
Seeds are black in their deep sockets, and another
Shrivelling moon

Half-lights the calmer times of indecision,
Rain damps down the summer's middle-class ambition,
And very soon

A stale and unconvinced denial of defeat
Mutters with pauses from the elder hedge its weak
Self-pitying tune:

Toads pause, the handsome slugs will hide
And the caught bee dry and fade inside
The emptied room.

Meeting by the Gjulika Meadow

He had in his hand a red plant
picked near the snow under
the suspicious frontier, when we met
by the Gjulika meadow.

And he spoke slowly in English,
and the black thunder bucked about
and the hard rain decidedly hit
round the broken hut,

And he made a fire, the Slovene
with the off-white face,
where it was dry still under
the pines, and he took

Out a black and bent copper
coffee-pot, and sugar, and
garlic and bread. And the rain-drops
fried in the fire

And we were warm in our
wetness and sipped at the very
hot coffee (the Slovene
learnt his English at Boston)

And talked under the thunder
about Europe, about dealing
in furs, about thunder, about
rain, and invisible trout

In the silk-blue Sava,
About Europe again, and frontiers.

His Zagreb boots were thin: and
he was taking the plant

Picked by the snow under the
nervous frontier to his lovely
daughter underneath in the farm,
who was crippled

By her mother's sin (what sin?),
he said. We talked of Europe,
Europe; and the immature frogs
slipped in the wet grass.

The thunder was sneering, and
in the lower woods we enjoyed
the lemon sun again, and the scent
and magenta of cyclamens.

Ivy Smothers the Bank

Yet through the other window
such oddments shine
as a white lupin planted

by a shed, a white horse
against the brown
matt-surface of the down.

Pretend these win,
pretend the ivy loses.

The Tune

My familiars visit the romantic caves,
the 1830 mansions and the Coade Stone lion,
dive into the stump-speckled valley of Hafod,
read Rogers on the robin, under the weed-
surrounded urn.

Where they go, brambles bridge the ha-ha,
joining, at last, exploited nature
to the uncultivated garden. Black leaves slime up
the ornamental water, and choke the pipe to
the crusted fountain. And the black-budded ash

Splits the Gothic summer-house, *Anno Pacis*
on the obelisk, written
a hundred years too soon. Click, and the camera,
in a technique of corn and apples,
records them

For smooth paper, with black sky, deep shadow
and shine. But my friend the Russian
from Galicia curls
a lip and sings near midnight
to the microphone
some song of the deep and
unrestricted bed,

with the humpbacked trumpeter, the octoroon, the
pneumothorax cases beating out insistently
the tune.

Brilliant Flowers on a
White Plate, at Breakfast

Duncovitch the philosopher
Lived in a barrel throughout winter,
In spring and summer was head waiter,
Entered, town-crying 'Marmalada!',
Laid on your plate alone – quite right,
Since you were like a picture – purple
Curved anthers of the Caper.

O Brown Legged Bristol Ladies

Brown legged Bristol ladies
 Forgive if I offend you,
And proffer some advice
 In hopes to mend you.

Upon your brown backs lie more gaily,
Your warm years live more frailly,
And take what luck may lend you.

Shut not your mouths so tightly,
On your long feet walk more lightly,
More in the middle bend you.

Contempt of scented lotions
And young old-maidish notions –
Ah, these you think commend you.

But if your cramped emotions
Rise up and scream like oceans
And like a bomb blast rend you,

If 'Sweet, how like you this?'
Inform your graver kiss,
Your living may befriend you.

But if you will not kiss,
And if you take no risk,
And sourly fade unblissed,
May hairiest chins extend you.

 O brown legged Bristol ladies,
  Forgive if this offend you,
 Such good advice, I know,
  Never will mend you.

May Trees in a Storm

How this year of years do I best see
These famous blossoms of the dangerous May?

In headlights wild and scattering,
Threshing in a wind of May?

    The four roads join.
  HALT glitters, but I choose
      Your way.

The Chandeliers

For you, love's chandeliers are lit.
In this pleasure dome's pavilion
These golden snakes from every slit
Proclaim, proclaim untrue, untrue,
But not to you for whom
    These brightest chandeliers are lit.

For you, for you in violet
And green, red-lipped
And little fingered and for your
Small quizzing face
From brushed back hair do I declare
    These chandeliers of love are lit.

We've paid our fee. And thanks to it
Have gone from room to rose-red room,
Have watched the Indian lotus spread,
Kissed beside the Chinese bed,
Crossed again the roped-in hall
And from this door
By fear, delight, amazement gripped
Have seen once more
How all for you, for you, and all for you,
    These brightest chandeliers are lit.

Bibliotheca Bodleiana

Edwardus Comes Clarendoniae
Clamped to his niche by an iron brace
Lifts to the white mercy of sparrows
His foppish foolish face.

Primus Angliae Cancellarius,
He's joined the race of stone.
I belong still to your race
Of warm mouth and bone.

Bibliotheca Bodleiana,
My library is love for a while.
O Illuminatio mea, I wait
For your entering smile.

Slowly the Mule Goes Up

Slowly the mule goes up,
One of the millions of men
Loosely bestrides it.
Another mule panniered with sacks
Climbs ahead and ahead.

   Black cinders they loosen
   Trickle toward me.

They are lost in the blaze
Of the fennel,
Emerge, and climb on to the ridge.
They show for a moment. They stay.

Outlined upon all of the blue.

   And they cross, the two beasts,
   And the sacks, and the man.
     And entirely
   Are lost to my view.

To the Neckar

(From the German of Hölderlin)

Your glens provoked my heart to life.
  Around me played your ripples and of all
    The gracious hills which know you, wanderer,
      Not one is strange to me.

The breeze of heaven on your peaks has often
  Freed me of subjection's pain. Life out
    Of joy's goblet, from the valley shone
      The bluish silver of your wave.

The mountain springs run down to you, my heart
  Runs with them and you take us both
    To the still grandeur of the Rhine, down
      To its cities and enlivening isles.

But yet the world delights me. Longing
  For the charms of earth my eye escapes to Smyrna's
    Coast, to Ilion's wood, to golden
      Pactolus. Repeatedly I'd land

At Sunium too, and ask the tongueless path, Olympion,
  For your colonnades! Before antiquity and gale
    Thick in the rubble of Athenian temples
      And their gods enshrine you too,

Who've stood so long there and alone, O pride
  Of a world which now exists no more.
    And O you fairest islands
      Of Ionia, where the sea wind

Cools the hot shore, then whispers
   Through the wood of laurels when the sunlight
      Warms the vine, ah, where a golden autumn changes
         The sighs of poor men into songs,

When its pomegranates ripen, oranges
   In green night wink, and mastic
      Drips its gum, and kettle drum and cymbal
         Beat to the dance's labyrinth.

To you, O islands, O to you my tutelary god
   One day may bring me. Lovely with meadows
      And with willowed banks my river here
         Meanwhile stays true to me.

The Critics

'Poems, beyond his scope
Or his or hers?'

'Yes, picked clean
Of echoes, pathos,
Clichés of heart and head, and
Other small hard
Obstinate burrs.'

'Those are the most free
Poems that we mean.'

'And have
Most seldom seen.'

Après la Chasse

In Memory of Maurice Beaubrun

Repent. Why? Not a kingdom of
heaven is at hand
where a for once clement king,
viz. otherwise a colonel, absolute,
will check, perhaps, if you do,
if you trust his promises,
his electric torturer's clean hand.

Repent. Yes, enough. But not
because you fear a punishment, or
being shut out. Too late for that.
Repent? Admit at least in pursuit
you went often too far.
Also, in the fairground in the distorting
true mirror hesitated to recognize

Sufficiently what you are,
who are not genius or saint also.
Repent, but not too much,
no grub by grub crawling in white. Old
friend, the kingdom, soviet, democracy – no,
the small mild hamlet of free
felicity, brief, is not of such.

A Painter of Our Day

He teaches me what is: never nostalgia,
Yet never contempt for what has been composed.
With 'strangle the swan' I sympathize:
He would not paint a swan or a rose.
I would not write them. He says don't disregard
The single swan drawing a glittering circumflex
Along your river avenue: look – *Allons*
Voir si la rose? – No, but into
Its packed centre. Recognizing there much
Old reiterated wisdom of perceiving?
No, seeing what you see: what is.

At Verneuil, round Thérèse of Lisieux
After her first communion (but 'she' is
A whiteness in the light and shadow)
Maurice Denis has woven roses (but they
Are shape, in a selection of the curves
That roses in a small back garden here
Are made to take, among the shadows
And the lights). M. le Curé says –
The dull historian of ideas, dull
Courtauld lecturer says – seldom what is,
Which is for each of us. I do not say transfer,
Translate, transplant, transpose, only accept the old
Swan of snow; again, the rose whose pink contains
A blue, if either comes my way.

This my old friend teaches me. I say, I see
This, that, in your abstract pictures, he says
Not quite no. I say, This blue space is that small
Window in your studio or is Atlantic Penwith,
Through a dolmen, blue. Slightly he shrugs away.

I say, The title says. He says, I find the titles
Afterwards. Titles are difficult: suggest a title
For this picture here. Children need names,
I must reflect, and I am taught again to accept
What is; also, that always each wonderful realm
He makes and the immense realm each other penetrate.

Yet of the few painters, or few poets, each
Of us can live by, most have been
Long dead: they are Collected Works,
Their Retrospective, their Memorial
Exhibition all the time is here.
The centre of them, where they most exist, in
Freedom, has to accept each friend, each devotee.
Suddenly when young or in our first ability
We find them, slowly we find the reasons
For our love, finding ourselves, and what we lack
As well or need the most. It is about this,
This centre, historians of art or poetry
Cook their most tedious fudge, missing
Or smearing each realm-maker's liberty; it is the real,
Like you, who win, against art's pedants,
Art's officials, and art's auctioneers: innocent
You say your first Cumbrian landscapes were
As my small girl, who swopped her puns with you,
Seeing them again – 'after 50 (500) years'
You write – in Bâle. I saw innocent
Pictures by you first: and you once showed
Me, reproduced, Raphael's Three Graces, not to say
Pink and pure white spiralling pencils that
I find again each June in striped petunias.

Last year you threw a ball, loving its line of
Sheer, rebounding curves, in light,

You spoke in the long room floating
Above the lake of Raphael, Giorgione, Tobey,
Braque, Cézanne, of blue, and of discovery, and
Of the power of lasting like Cézanne, in art,
To the extreme end: with age combining
Unimaginable Giorgione's youth I watched you,
Watched your pictures (in which stronger innocence
For the organized above all accident survives),
Heard you, in your centre again, saddened
By leaving you and by your physical age,
And by the snow and sleet after your sunshine
Round the Alpine train.

                    Then days, days after
Were irradiated round me by your truth.

Trôo

About Owls

Autumnal, and by day,
An owl's round cry,
As if old, or not well,
Hesitating to an un-

Certain thread, as if
Conscious, a most soft
Collapse of feathers
It might soon

Fall dead –
As if there were
Irreconcilable
Policies of conscious

Owls, a curtain
Between owls, propaganda
And prestige
Of owls, sustained

Unkindness of owls
To owls, even
In the night; which
Is not to say

If owls live
In an owl moment
Alone, it is
Emptied of delight.

Poem in Briefest Prose

My dear, about sunsets (which this is about) nowadays we cannot rhyme or talk in rhythm. Sunsets, at the time I make this note, are *vieux jeu* for poets. And critics would not like them. Of course, they are right. Who is to be congratulated on sunsets? Who is responsible, I mean, for sunsets after all?

Still, walking under our long hills and thinking, since women – who is responsible for them? – lose no appeal, of you, this evening's display, you cleanse my eyes so much, has to be mentioned.

Float, for example,

(You see I now break up the lines)

Between the upper sky's light cream of peppermint

(And I use a few capitals)

and this great field

THREE CLOUDS:

They are so gay, that is the epithet.

(This is still prose, my dear)

They are – shall I pretend –

THREE BALLOONS

Of Striped Silk

released (let us rejoin the lines) in the eighteenth century, still with the Terror to come.

Clumps of trees, too, along with the hill crest, planted to the order of the brewer's young wife who was painted exquisitely by an artist who spoke of the foolishness of sunsets, are so exceedingly now solid and black, upon the ormer shell, in the east, of a lower sky.

Something else he and she never saw, also occurs. It belongs to our sunsetting, to us also entirely, I mean to you and me. A vapour trail, now, is drawn by a plane too small to observe, across, and inside (capitals tempt me again) the Most Luminous Patch. It is

Fire, across Fire
ending in feathers, or in smoke, of
luminous brown.

Why the plane is there, allow me to overlook. I will say that in ten minutes or less the trail will be Rose, or else Scarlet, my dear one, no comet so grand.

Scent of Women

Peculiar the scent of wood anemones,
they smell like sweat of aestuous women,
bitter, green. Each year I enter
a copse where these fox-flowers grow.

For their exquisiteness I go, then
think of women I never loved, and feared,
too soon thinking of the cyclamen.

On Migration

On that spare grass, by that sparse wood –
For some reason or none
I had driven you there.

I dare say you were beautiful.
I did not see it,
And I did not care.

You were expecting love,
I did not give it;
My object felt – not recognized – elsewhere,
I came down on your cornice;
And I rested there.

Splendid you were. And I repeat,
I did not see it,
Admit again I did not care.
That puzzled me, not knowing then
Why I was there.

Bird of Six a.m.

A reedy robin of September,
Most invisible early bird,
Sings through the curl
And the heat of the mist, and I move:

And I think
Of the sweat on the white
Of her cheek last night
When she slightly
Turned to be kissed.

Much doubt, much doubt
He is threading and concentrating
In his reedy
Insistent twist,
Coming up to my six a.m. ear,
Most melancholy early bird
Out of the heat of the mist.

Singing

I heard you in the next room singing,
The notes were you.
'With gaiety and lightness she runs up',
I thought, 'a delicate newel stair,
And hovers there, and hovers there.'

I could not see you. I could hear:
You moved about, stood by the window,
By the mirror, raised your foot to a chair,
You went on singing; were – I heard,
Still hear – pure notes by now,
Your underfeathers stirred
On the warm
Current of upholding air.

Heart Burial

They fetched it along, and they slipped it in,
Mr Hardy's heart in a biscuit tin.

Mrs Hardy said, This grave is my bed
And my husband Thomas was not well-bred.

And the heart spoke up, and it mildly said,
Give me to my old dog Wessex instead,

Give me to my surly old Wessex instead,
But Wessex was busy with a fresh sheep's head,

And the rector pretended he did not hear,
And dry was the sexton and needed beer,

And bumpetty bump and din din din
Earth fell on the box and the biscuit tin.

Career of a Sharp-Profiled Public Servant

He tied himself to four umbrellas
and jumped – admittedly it was not high –
from the E.E. tower of his father's church.

He rolled, feet together, hands tight to each side,
over primroses to the edge of the cliff on his father's glebe
and stopped – exactly – 3 inches from

a fall of 200 feet. He was imprisoned
in the Russian Revolution, and came home
and to test that nerve

climbed to the top of the steel-framed
mile-measurer above that cliff, and stood there
as before, on one foot, in the high wind,

and he became, the *manes* of our house-master
will learn with relief, the most conventional
pimp of the Crown,

and was ennobled.

The Swing

The empty swing in the garden
  Moves backwards, forwards,

Back, then forward,
Hidden a moment by its tree trunk
On each diminishing sway,
Our child who swung there crying
Having slipped off, and gone away.

A New Tree

It is April, she is held
to the window
to see leaves of our new
weeping willow, less

green than a yellow:
I love what she is; and
may be – that she gives,
and is given, so lives

now, and again
in a heaven;
there will be heavy
absence of light

and cold rain,
but I love
in her that at times
the quick drops

should catch light
down the pane, a sun
being fiercely
let loose again.

Coincidence of 10 p.m.

A scent of quinces and a lunar bow –
A *donnée*, so the smart reviewers say –
What should be done with it I do not know,
A scent of quinces and a lunar bow.

Saint-Jacques

Note on Grünewald

Even if ten of my poems should be read in ten hundred years
    time,
I'd sooner, kind readers thank you, myself
be around, in spite of aspirations and all
pious aere perennius asseverations, to sniff
in the month appropriate as once
for instance in the hot street with-
in distance of Grünewald's spotted green-rotted Christ,
            the scent of the flowers of lime.

So I join, at least today, morning of glitter in December,
our poet Cowper, who decided as he watched the leaves of
his whole county falling in a shower of yellow,
that shortness of staying in this Vale of Tears, for all
his madness and his swingeing fears, ceased
to attract him: he would leave this world never,
he would enjoy, in spite of idealisms and moral realisms,
            the good of it for ever, and ever.

To a Poet's Biographer

Find out what boy he was, how
His unrecognized needs were fed,
What rocks his brilliant redstarts flickered from,
Feel for the slag or bilberry bank that held his head.

Enter his blue Eden by this grace. Then
His young and later Hell. Remembering
You do not grind a felling axe in your
Green limestone dell; and that you wish him well.

One Remained

So we travelled together again
By the train down the valley,
On top of the water reflecting
Blackness and green,
I in the carriage. And you –

I walked up through the trees,
Slept guilty and badly, woke up
To customary echoes, heard sadly
Expected music of hens,
In the hollows.

And you? Men I once knew
Climbed up to muffle the clappers,
Descended to swing
Slow-seeming peals for an hour,
Sun-veils holding the tower.

To begin with slightly it rained.
Bright-feathered hens
Were shooed out, and
Returned. There it was
You remained.

Louis MacNeice

2 September 1963

I turned on the transistor:
By luck, for your sorrel,
Your *Vol de Nuit*,
It was Haydn,

Black and diffident man
Of the bog and the stoa
Whose rush of love
Was rejected,

Whose wolfhound
Bent round my table,
Who are no longer around
In your Chinese

Garden of poems.
Where one is of water,
On which tea-yellow
Leaves of another

Are falling, always
Are falling, this one
Is a stone by itself,
On which you inscribe

With invisible legible letters
That unrest of the soul
Which you found
So wryly appalling.

You have gone: will
No longer arrange
In sunlight with wit
Your aloneness.

But, classical quizzical
One, whose scent is
Sharp in the centre,
Your garden is open.

Wild Doves Arriving, and Absorbed in Hedges

There is a contrast between the high flight of doves
And their douce behaviour two by two in hedges.
They fly in parties. Their wings are sharp and quick and nervy.
They have purpose. Their quick flight pauses, doves drop
    away
In ones for now new green of hedges, where flight from branch
To branch inside is nothing wild. Mated, their ringed
Eyes, their melody, are mild. 'Dove-grey', we say, 'dove-
    grey.'
At times they walk for smoothness on quiet roads.
A car approaches. Spreading white tails they rise
And are once more invisibly absorbed in hedges.

No Sprinkling of Bright Weeds

Earth – that old-hat phrase of superseded days –
goes red with my slack-satin flowers,
my poppies; my cornflowers of absolute blue –
both mix into my wheat. Also out of the ears

with which it's level, stares each sepal-criss-
crossed flat corncockle eye,
magenta, without a blink the whole
day into the hot sky.

   Lady, not now. Lady in whose gay
bleached hair were ears of wheat with poppies if not corn-
flowers and cockles mixed, and in your south love-
in-the-mist and black-pupilled scarlet pheasant's eye,

Sunburned Ceres, you must understand (you catch my
tone) that now across all plains – no longer fields –
your very carefully treated wheat must be
a clean stand for maximated yields.

Our bodily, of course our economic and our
advertising needs
permit, Lady, except among peasants backward on thin soil,
no sprinkling of bright weeds.

Encouragement, on a Leaf

Written on a gold leaf in Greek
    Take Courage –
and we who survived placed the leaf
under your hands, so that without
all loss of hope you might meet indifferent
Charon, and cross the cold Styx.

Friend, things have changed. Charon we meet,
the cold river flows through our lives. If,
as we shut you away, if
you could pass out to ourselves in your grey
claw from your peace
the gold leaf on which
Take Courage is written.

The Gods and the Colonels

If one saw an actual snake
wreathing through an actual
skull's eye.

Instead I arrange such a tableau
with a rubber viper and a badger's skull
and have left it on the spare
room window sill.

And somewhere cold
clear water flows under
pink oleanders of
Theocritus –

whom I should, I think, now
spell Theokritos, *de novo*,
judge of the gods, accent
on the i –

without
cutting of the throat
of a white kid. But

the gods and the colonels
whom they serve, the whole
time insist
on blood.

Note from Bruegel

What fat mushroom face,
Neckless, lurks visibly behind the still
Leafless twig-work of this
April's elders, by the broken barn?

What even now squat rounded
Vessel, with a wide flat
Snub nose, a wider, greedy, ominous
Most senseless grin,

Usurps that ground?
'He who eats fire, shits sparks'
And in a new way our sky now
Threatens to rain down its larks.

Nazareth Pitcher

Nazareth Pitcher, in
My family book I
Notice your name, married, in
Hingham, East Anglia,

Settled in Hingham, New England,
Under your old English rector,
Despoiler of churches, a
'Violent schismatic'.

After bearing your children,
So far from the moral
Sloth of the Yare
You were the husk of a seed

Stranded out there, –
Of a dock, no, I suppose
Of a burr thrown aside by
A lift of the tide

On to that god-awful glacier-
Ground ghost of a coast,
Ninety-one
When you died.

Admire you? I doubt it,
Not liking pride
Of your kind in original sin;
Suspecting as well, Nazareth,

Your lips were too thin –
And since we are nuclear sinners,
That you might be pleased
By the mess we are in.

Respect to Pluto

Whatever sent the drie Arabia
Breathes from her spices on the morning grey
May perfume, if I wish, my scentless day:

Open or close my eyes,
Spices may crackle, the new born bird may rise
In scattering brilliance through these greyer skies,

If I am wise. Though I deplore the rape,
I'm glad, among the sub-fusc violets, at my escape,
And pay respect to Pluto in his crêpe.

The Cyprian's Spring

The Cyprian's Spring by water only can be
reached, your pedalo moored to a hole in rock
on the slight slap of violet water. Press
your right shoulder to tearing rock along
a narrow path, brush the magenta
of wild gladioli, enter shadow, before which
also pomegranates flower. Swallows fly out,
the Cyprian's Spring breaks out, so many bright
gallons per cool minute, so many bright
gallons per cool hour, so many gallons
per cool century, so many glittering gallons
per cool aeon.

              Swallows fly in, fly out,
in wild figs overhead are doves. Wet ferns
of black filaments slenderer
than the Cyprian's secret hair move
in the water breeze.

           Come here alone,
there is no room for two.

           Back in the arrogant
sun, if you upset your pedalo, and tumble
in, expect sharp stinging of purplish-
black sea-urchin spines.

Raw Ream: Remembering, Now Dead,
a Teacher

I speak of times before high whining of cars or round
growling of planes, when silence was fashioned by noises:
it is a pool in our hollow of pines looped by the sun
which makes them the colour of foxes, is defined
lightly by crows passing over, by
a huckling of hens relieved of their eggs,
by women calling to women, is broken, so
made by clangs, or by regular bells now and then.

Carrying white eggs for payment
I walk to you over the green
to learn reading, hearing this
sunshine of silence. Minnie, I say, these eggs
are my money. You laugh, take the eggs
(which you will give back to my mother),
skin ream off a pan, spread for me honey
on bread, yellow ream over honey.

Return to Florence

A theatre-sky, of navy blue, at night:
traffic of the night, it darts, it screams,
it is straight swifts of night with lighted
eyes: upwards I read on a new building's

Face, Here P. B. Shelley wrote
Ode to the West Wind. Your poet, no. Nor
mine, yet say *wĭnd* as he will or *wīnd,*
oh, I say *willkommen, welcome, ben-*

Venuto, oh, *bienvenu;* and I – I am
here again, after fourteen years: I-you.
I-you shall in a minute see the Duomo's
domino sides enormous up into the night,

I-you shall past *our* latteria stroll – there,
that corner shop where, look – for your
sake – the kind man scented my hair. Soon
must Il Bianco come into view,

The Loggia lighted, Dante again in the night,
reading, on walls. I-you. Sleeping. To swifts
of morning tomorrow waking. Dead and to come,
oh, *welcome, willkommen, benvenuti,* oh, *bienvenus!*

The Dying of a Long Lost Lover

Your mother slept with me – I daresay you regard that
as peculiar, I daresay she is old (and so am I,
but I'm less your affair). Think. She was young.
Imagine her. I see still her long fingers round her belt.

Which is her myth, her past, or her reality?
Young, did not foretell this old I do not know.
I know she is the hand which stroked both me and you:
various the occasions, and the kinds, of love she felt.

You touch that vehicle of extinct heat. But love
that she loved, and was the call of love. With some
distaste you soon may close her eyes: love
that I see her young long fingers at her belt.

The Chapel

This being one of the days for me
When the word death tolls, I find
The chapel of O Spes Unica
I've driven to see is closed;

In which, on black touch, a poet
Of a poet says 'I was his friend.'
For whatever reason, because a boy
Yesterday smashed off a staid

Effigy's alabaster toes, or because
Today the verger's dead or to his
Married daughter in Nottingham goes, I say
The chapel of O Spes Unica is closed.

The Oculi

I said, Your boat is animal,
These are his eyes, he finds a way
With them.

No, you said, the Goddess
Of Launching – if we pray –
Is in the prow. These are her eyes, then:
She comes, she sees, in a swart night,
Down, up, over, again down
Exceptional waves,
With her two eyes – if our prayer-mind is right –
Lent from her head. For our boat, she only
Sees, and we then are comforted.

I said, I have no goddess, no god either,
Inside my head. You said, It's practical,
And shook your head.

These blank lime-whitish
Eyes, defined by lines of black,
Upon the yellow and the red.

Travelling at Night

(After Tu Fu)

Delicate grasses ashore
stir in a small wind. Tall
my boat's mast in this
night's loneliness. Stars
depend to these
wide wide levels.

A moon dances on this great
river's rippling.

Writing gives me no name,
illness, age, bar my advancement –
drifting, drifting
here, what am I like
but a tern of the sandbanks
in between earth
and heaven?

Consolation Obvious, Old Hat, I Admit, Not Proper, Not Entire

Trees which are light and free in the spring
Become fat lard-bags in dull green,
But then change to brown,
And their dry leaves drift down.

But

O to dry never,
To lay bright girls for ever.

EDWIN MUIR

Horses

Those lumbering horses in the steady plough,
On the bare field – I wonder why, just now,
They seemed terrible, so wild and strange,
Like magic power on the stony grange.

Perhaps some childish hour has come again,
When I watched fearful, through the blackening rain,
Their hooves like pistons in an ancient mill
Move up and down, yet seem as standing still.

Their conquering hooves which trod the stubble down
Were ritual that turned the field to brown,
And their great hulks were seraphim of gold,
Or mute ecstatic monsters on the mould.

And oh the rapture, when, one furrow done,
They marched broad-breasted to the sinking sun!
The light flowed off their bossy sides in flakes;
The furrows rolled behind like struggling snakes.

But when at dusk with steaming nostrils home
They came, they seemed gigantic in the gloam,
And warm and glowing with mysterious fire
That lit their smouldering bodies in the mire.

Their eyes as brilliant and as wide as night
Gleamed with a cruel apocalyptic light.
Their manes the leaping ire of the wind
Lifted with rage invisible and blind.

Ah, now it fades! it fades! and I must pine
Again for that dread country crystalline,
Where the blank field and the still-standing tree
Were bright and fearful presences to me.

Hölderlin's Journey

When Hölderlin started from Bordeaux
   He was not mad but lost in mind,
For time and space had fled away
   With her he had to find.

'The morning bells rang over France
   From tower to tower. At noon I came
Into a maze of little hills,
   Head-high and every hill the same.

'A little world of emerald hills,
   And at their heart a faint bell tolled;
Wedding or burial, who could say?
   For death, unseen, is bold.

'Too small to climb, too tall to show
   More than themselves, the hills lay round.
Nearer to her, or farther? They
   Might have stretched to the world's bound.

'A shallow candour was their all,
   And the mean riddle, How to tally
Reality with such appearance,
   When in the nearest valley

'Perhaps already she I sought,
   She, sought and seeker, had gone by,
And each of us in turn was trapped
   By simple treachery.

'The evening brought a field, a wood.
   I left behind the hills of lies,

And watched beside a mouldering gate
  A deer with its rock-crystal eyes.

'On either pillar of the gate
  A deer's head watched within the stone.
The living deer with quiet look
  Seemed to be gazing on

'Its pictured death – and suddenly
  I knew, Diotima was dead,
As if a single thought had sprung
  From the cold and the living head.

'That image held me and I saw
  All moving things so still and sad,
But till I came into the mountains
  I know I was not mad.

'What made the change? The hills and towers
  Stood otherwise than they should stand,
And without fear the lawless roads
  Ran wrong through all the land.

'Upon the swarming towns of iron
  The bells hailed down their iron peals,
Above the iron bells the swallows
  Glided on iron wheels.

'And there I watched in one confounded
  The living and the unliving head.
Why should it be? For now I know
  Diotima was dead

'Before I left the starting place;
  Empty the course, the garland gone,

And all that race as motionless
  As these two heads of stone.'

So Hölderlin mused for thirty years
  On a green hill by Tübingen,
Dragging in pain a broken mind
  And giving thanks to God and men.

The Fall

What shape had I before the Fall?
  What hills and rivers did I seek?
What were my thoughts then? And of what
  Forgotten histories did I speak

To my companions? Did our eyes
  From their foredestined watching-place
See Heaven and Earth one land, and range
  Therein through all of Time and Space?

Did I see Chaos and the Word,
  The suppliant Dust, the moving Hand,
Myself, the Many and the One,
  The dead, the living Land?

That height cannot be scaled again.
  My fall was like the fall that burst
Old Lear's heart on the summer sward.
  Where I lie now I stood at first.

The ancient pain returns anew.
  Where was I ere I came to man?
What shape among the shapes that once
  Agelong through endless Eden ran?

Did I see there the dragon brood
  By streams their emerald scales unfold,
While from their amber eyeballs fell
  Soft-rayed the rustling gold?

It must be that one time I walked
  By rivers where the dragon drinks;
But this side Eden's wall I meet
  On every twisting road the Sphinx

Whose head is like a wooden prow
   That forward leaning dizzily
Over the seas of whitened worlds
   Has passed and nothing found to see,

Whose breast, a flashing ploughshare, once
   Cut the rich furrows wrinkled in
Venusberg's sultry underworld
   And busy trampled fields of sin,

Whose salt-white brow like crusted fire
   Smiles ever, whose cheeks are red as blood,
Whose dolphin back is flowered yet
   With wrack that swam upon the Flood.

Since then in antique attitudes
   I swing the bright two-handed sword
And strike and strike the marble brow,
   Wide-eyed and watchful as a bird,

Smite hard between the basilisk eyes,
   And carve the snaky dolphin side,
Until the coils are cloven in two
   And free the glittering pinions glide.

Like quicksilver the scales slip down,
   Upon the air the spirit flies,
And so I build me Heaven and Hell
   To buy my bartered Paradise.

While from a legendary height
   I see a shadowy figure fall,
And not far off another beats
   With his bare hands on Eden's wall.

Merlin

O Merlin in your crystal cave
Deep in the diamond of the day,
Will there ever be a singer
Whose music will smooth away
The furrow drawn by Adam's finger
Across the meadow and the wave?
Or a runner who'll outrun
Man's long shadow driving on,
Break through the gate of memory
And hang the apple on the tree?
Will your magic ever show
The sleeping bride shut in her bower,
The day wreathed in its mound of snow
And Time locked in his tower?

The Unfamiliar Place

I do not know this place,
Though here for long I have run
My changing race
In the moon and the sun,
Within this wooded glade
Far up the mountainside
Where Christ and Caesar died
And the first man was made.

I have seen this turning light
For many a day.
I have not been away
Even in dreams of the night.
In the unnumbered names
My fathers gave these things
I seek a kingdom lost,
Sleeping with folded wings.
I have questioned many a ghost
Far inland in my dreams,
Enquired of fears and shames
The dark and winding way
To the day within my day.

And aloft I have stood
And given my eyes their fill,
Have watched the bad and the good
Go up and down the hill,
The peasants on the plain
Ploughing the fields red,
The roads running alone,
The ambush in the wood,
The victim walking on,

The misery-blackened door
That never will open again,
The tumblers at the fair,
The watchers on the stair,
Cradle and bridal-bed,
The living and the dead
Scattered on every shore.

All this I have seen
Twice over, there and here,
Knocking at dead men's gates
To ask the living way,
And viewing this upper scene.
But I am balked by fear
And what my lips say
To drown the voice of fear.
The earthly day waits.

The Place of Light and Darkness

Walking on the harvest hills of Night
Time's elder brother, the great husbandman,
Goes on his ancient round. His massive lantern,
Simpler than the first fashion, lights the rows
Of stooks that lean like little golden graves
Or tasselled barges foundering low
In the black stream.

            He sees that all is ready,
The trees all stripped, the orchards bare, the nests
Empty. All things grown
Homeless and whole. He sees the hills of grain,
A day all yellow and red, flowers, fruit, and corn.
The soft hair harvest-golden in darkness.
Children playing
In the late night-black day of time. He sees
The lover standing by the trysting-tree
Who'll never find his love till all are gathered
In light or darkness. The unnumbered living
Numbered and bound and sheaved.

              O could that day
Break on this side of time!

             A wind shakes
The loaded sheaves, the feathery tomb bursts open,
And yellow hair is poured along the ground
From the bent neck of time. The woods cry:
This is the resurrection.

O little judgment days lost in the dark,
Seen by the bat and screech-owl!

             He goes on,
Bearing within his ocean-heart the jewel,
The day all yellow and red wherein a sun
Shines on the endless harvest lands of time.

To J. F. H. (1897-1934)

Shot from the sling into the perilous road,
The hundred mile long hurtling bowling alley,
Today I saw you pass full tilt for the jack.
Or it seemed a race beyond time's gate you rode,
Trussed to the motor cycle, shoulder and head
Fastened to flying fate, so that your back
Left nothing but a widening wake of dumb
Scornful oblivion. It was you, yet some
Soft finger somewhere turned a different day,
The day I left you in that narrow valley,
Close to my foot, but already far away;
And I remembered you were seven years dead.

Yet you were there so clearly, I could not tell
For a moment in the hot still afternoon
What world I walked in, since it held us two,
A dead and a living man. Had I cracked the shell
That hides the secret souls, had I fallen through,
I idly wondered, and in so falling found
The land where life's untraceable truants run
Hunting a halting stage? Was this the ground
That stretched beyond the span-wide world-wide ditch,
So like the ground I knew, yet so unlike,
Because it said 'Again', all this again,
The flying road, the motionless house again,
And, stretched between, the tension of your face –
As you ran in dust the burning comet's race
Athirst for the ease of ash – the eating itch
To be elsewhere, nowhere, the driving pain
Clamping the shoulders back? Was death's low dike
So easy to leap as this and so commonplace,
A jump from here through here straight into here,

An operation to make you what you were
Before, no better or worse? And yet the fear?

The clock-hand moved, the street slipped into its place,
Two cars went by. A chance face flying past
Had started it all and made a hole in space,
The hole you looked through always. I knew at last
The sight you saw there, the terror and mystery
Of unrepeatable life so plainly given
To you half wrapped still in eternity,
Who had come by such a simple road from heaven;
So that you did not need to have the story
Retold, or bid the heavy world turn again,
But felt the terror of the trysting place,
The crowning test, the treachery and the glory.

The Wayside Station

Here at the wayside station, as many a morning,
I watch the smoke torn from the fumy engine
Crawling across the field in serpent sorrow.
Flat in the east, held down by stolid clouds,
The struggling day is born and shines already
On its warm hearth far off. Yet something here
Glimmers along the ground to show the seagulls
White on the furrows' black unturning waves.

But now the light has broadened.
I watch the farmstead on the little hill,
That seems to mutter: 'Here is day again'
Unwillingly. Now the sad cattle wake
In every byre and stall,
The ploughboy stirs in the loft, the farmer groans
And feels the day like a familiar ache
Deep in his body, though the house is dark.
The lovers part
Now in the bedroom where the pillows gleam
Great and mysterious as deep hills of snow,
An inaccessible land. The wood stands waiting
While the bright snare slips coil by coil around it,
Dark silver on every branch. The lonely stream
That rode through darkness leaps the gap of light,
Its voice grown loud, and starts its winding journey
Through the day and time and war and history.

The Human Fold

Here penned within the human fold
No longer now we shake the bars,
Although the ever-moving stars
Night after night in order rolled
Rebuke this stationary farce.
There's no alternative here but love,
So far as genuine love can be
Where there's no genuine liberty
To give or take, to lose or have,
And having rots with wrong, and loss
Itself has no security
Except in the well-managed grave,
And all we do is done to prove
Content and discontent both are gross.
Yet sometimes here we still can see
The dragon with his tears of gold,
The bat-browed sphinx
Shake loose her wings
That have no hold and fan no air,
All struck dead by her stare.
Hell shoots its avalanche at our feet,
In heaven the souls go up and down,
And we can see from this our seat
The heavenly and the hellish town,
The green cross growing in a wood
Close by old Eden's crumbling wall,
And God Himself in full manhood
Riding against the Fall.
All this; but here our sight is bound
By ten dull faces in a round,
Each with a made-to-measure glance
That is in misery till it's found.

Yet looking at each countenance
I read this burden in them all:
'I lean my cheek from eternity
For time to slap, for time to slap.
I gather my bones from the bottomless clay
To lay my head in the light's lap.'

By what long way, by what dark way,
From what unpredetermined place,
Did we creep severally to this hole
And bring no memory and no grace
To furnish evidence of the soul,
Though come of an ancient race?
All gone, where now we cannot say,
Altar and shrine and boundary stone,
And of the legends of our day
This one remains alone:
'They loved and might have loved for ever,
But public trouble and private care
Faith and hope and love can sever
And strip the bed and the altar bare'.
Forward our towering shadows fall
Upon the naked nicheless wall,
And all we see is that shadow-dance.
Yet looking at each countenance
I read this burden in them all:
'I lean my cheek from eternity
For time to slap, for time to slap.
I gather my bones from the bottomless clay
To lay my head in the light's lap'.

The Face

See me with all the terrors on my roads,
The crusted shipwrecks rotting in my seas,
And the untroubled oval of my face
That alters idly with the moonlike modes
And is unfathomably framed to please
And deck the angular bone with passing grace.

I should have worn a terror-mask, should be
A sight to frighten hope and faith away,
Half charnel field, half battle and rutting ground.
Instead I am a smiling summer sea
That sleeps while underneath from bound to bound
The sun- and star-shaped killers gorge and play.

The Covenant

The covenant of god and animal,
The frieze of fabulous creatures winged and crowned,
And in the midst the woman and the man –

Lost long ago in fields beyond the Fall –
Keep faith in sleep-walled night and there are found
On our long journey back where we began.

Then the heraldic crest of nature lost
Shines out again until the weariless wave
Roofs with its sliding horror all that realm.

What jealousy, what rage could overwhelm
The golden lion and lamb and vault a grave
For innocence, innocence past defence or cost?

The Rider Victory

The rider Victory reins his horse
Midway across the empty bridge
As if head-tall he had met a wall.
Yet there was nothing there at all,
No bodiless barrier, ghostly ridge
To check the charger in his course
So suddenly, you'd think he'd fall.

Suspended, horse and rider stare
Leaping on air and legendary.
In front the waiting kingdom lies,
The bridge and all the roads are free;
But halted in implacable air
Rider and horse with stony eyes
Uprear their motionless statuary.

Epitaph

Into the grave, into the grave with him.
Quick, quick, with dust and stones this dead man cover
Who living was a flickering soul so dim
He was never truly loved nor truly a lover.

Since he was half and half, now let him be
Something entire at last here in this night
Which teaches us its absolute honesty
Who stay between the light and the half-light.

He scarce had room for sorrow, even his own;
His vastest dreams were less than six feet tall;
Free of all joys, he crept in himself alone:
To the grave with this poor image of us all.

If now is Resurrection, then let stay
Only what's ours when this is put away.

The Labyrinth

Since I emerged that day from the labyrinth,
Dazed with the tall and echoing passages,
The swift recoils, so many I almost feared
I'd meet myself returning at some smooth corner,
Myself or my ghost, for all there was unreal
After the straw ceased rustling and the bull
Lay dead upon the straw and I remained,
Blood-splashed, if dead or alive I could not tell
In the twilight nothingness (I might have been
A spirit seeking his body through the roads
Of intricate Hades) – ever since I came out
To the world, the still fields swift with flowers, the trees
All bright with blossom, the little green hills, the sea,
The sky and all in movement under it,
Shepherds and flocks and birds and the young and old,
(I stared in wonder at the young and the old,
For in the maze time had not been with me;
I had strayed, it seemed, past sun and season and change,
Past rest and motion, for I could not tell
At last if I moved or stayed; the maze itself
Revolved around me on its hidden axis
And swept me smoothly to its enemy,
The lovely world) – since I came out that day,
There have been times when I have heard my footsteps
Still echoing in the maze, and all the roads
That run through the noisy world, deceiving streets
That meet and part and meet, and rooms that open
Into each other – and never a final room –
Stairways and corridors and antechambers
That vacantly wait for some great audience,
The smooth sea-tracks that open and close again,
Tracks undiscoverable, indecipherable,

Paths on the earth and tunnels underground,
And bird-tracks in the air – all seemed a part
Of the great labyrinth. And then I'd stumble
In sudden blindness, hasten, almost run,
As if the maze itself were after me
And soon must catch me up. But taking thought,
I'd tell myself, 'You need not hurry. This
Is the firm good earth. All roads lie free before you.'
But my bad spirit would sneer, 'No, do not hurry.
No need to hurry. Haste and delay are equal
In this one world, for there's no exit, none,
No place to come to, and you'll end where you are,
Deep in the centre of the endless maze.'

I could not live if this were not illusion.
It is a world, perhaps; but there's another.
For once in a dream or trance I saw the gods
Each sitting on the top of his mountain-isle,
While down below the little ships sailed by,
Toy multitudes swarmed in the harbours, shepherds drove
Their tiny flocks to the pastures, marriage feasts
Went on below, small birthdays and holidays,
Ploughing and harvesting and life and death,
And all permissible, all acceptable,
Clear and secure as in a limpid dream.
But they, the gods, as large and bright as clouds,
Conversed across the sounds in tranquil voices
High in the sky above the untroubled sea,
And their eternal dialogue was peace
Where all these things were woven, and this our life
Was as a chord deep in that dialogue,
As easy utterance of harmonious words,
Spontaneous syllables bodying forth a world.

That was the real world; I have touched it once,
And now shall know it always. But the lie,
The maze, the wild-wood waste of falsehood, roads
That run and run and never reach an end,
Embowered in error – I'd be prisoned there
But that my soul has birdwings to fly free.

Oh these deceits are strong almost as life.
Last night I dreamt I was in the labyrinth,
And woke far on. I did not know the place.

The Journey Back

I

I take my journey back to seek my kindred,
Old founts dried up whose rivers run far on
Through you and me. Behind, the water-beds
Stone-white with drought; in front the riverless future
Through which our myriad tributaries will wander
When this live patchwork land of green and brown
With all its load of corn and weeds is withered.
But here, but here the water, clear or muddied.

Seek the beginnings, learn from whence you came,
And know the various earth of which you are made.
So I set out on this calm summer evening
From this my house and my father's. Looking back
I see that all behind is pined and shrunken,
The great trees small again, the good walls gone,
The road grown narrow and poor, wild heath and thorn
Where comfortable houses spread their gardens.
Only the sea and sky the same. But quiet
Deeper than I had breathed. Yet in this place,
Most strange and most familiar, my heart says
In a friend's voice, 'I beat in surety;'
My hands grow firm, my father's farmer hands,
And open and shut on surety while I walk
In patient trust. This is my father's gift
Left here for me at the first friendly station
On the long road.
                    But past it all is strange.
I must in other lives with many a leap
Blindfold, must lodge in dark and narrow skulls
With a few thoughts that pad from wall to wall

And never get out, must moulder in dusty hearts,
Inhabit many a dark or a sunny room,
Be in all things. And now I'm locked inside
The savage keep, the grim rectangular tower
From which the fanatic neighbour-hater scowls;
There all is emptiness and dirt and envy,
Dry rubbish of a life in anguish guarded
By mad and watchful eyes. From which I fall
To gasp and choke in the cramped miser's body
That winds its tightening winch to squeeze the soul
In a dry wooden box with slits for eyes.
And when I'm strangling there I flutter out
To drift like gossamer on the sunny wind,
A golden thistledown fool blown here and there,
Who for a lifetime scarcely knows a grief
Or thinks a thought. Then gasp in the hero's breast
That like a spring day in the northern seas
Is storm and shine and thunder all commingled,
A long-linked chain of lightning quenched in night.
Perhaps a murderer next. I watch those hands
That shall be always with me, serve my ends,
Button, unbutton for my body's needs,
Are intimate with me, the officious tools
That wash my face, push food into my mouth
Loathed servants fed from my averted heart.

So I usurp, grown avid for the end,
Body on body, am both father and child,
Causer and actor, spoiler and despoiled,
Robbing myself, myself, grinding the face
Of the poor, I poorest, who am both rich and poor,
Victor and victim, hapless Many in One.

In all these lives I have lodged, and each a prison.
I fly this prison to seek this other prison,

Impatient for the end – or the beginning
Before the walls were raised, the thick doors fastened,
And there was nothing but the breathing air,
Sun and soft grass, and sweet and vacant ease.
But there's no end, and I could break my journey
Now, here, without a loss, but that some day
I know I shall find a man who has done good
His long lifelong and is
Image of man from whom all have diverged.
The rest is hearsay. So I hie me back
To my sole starting-point, my random self
That in these rags and tatters clothes the soul.

2

Through countless wanderings,
Hastenings, lingerings,
From far I come,
And pass from place to place
In a sleep-wandering pace
To seek my home.

I wear the silver scars
Of blanched and dying stars
Forgotten long,
Whose consternations spread
Terror among the dead
And touched my song.

The well-bred animal
With coat of seemly mail
Was then my guide.
I trembled in my den
With all my kindred when
The dragon died.

Through forests wide and deep
I passed and as a sleep
My wandering was.
Before the word was said
With animal bowed head
I kept the laws.

I thread the shining day;
The mountains as in play
Dizzily turn
My wild road round and round.
No one has seen the ground
For which I burn.

Through countless wanderings,
Hastenings, lingerings,
Nearer I come,
In a sleep-wandering pace
To find the secret place
Where is my home.

3

And I remember in the bright light's maze
While poring on a red and rusted arrow
How once I laid my dead self in the barrow,
Closed my blank eyes and smoothed my face,
And stood aside, a third within that place,
And watched these two at their strange ritual,
And grieved for that day's deed so often done
When the poor child of man, leaving the sun,
Walks out into the sun and goes his way,
Not knowing the resurrection and the life,
Shut in his simple recurring day,

Familiar happiness and ordinary pain.
And while he lives content with child and wife
A million leaves, a million destinies fall,
And over and over again
The red rose blooms and moulders by the wall.

4

And sometimes through the air descends a dust
Blown from the scentless desert of dead time
That whispers: Do not put your trust
In the fed flesh, or colour, or sense, or shape.
This that I am you cannot gather in rhyme.
For once I was all
That you can name, a child, a woman, a flower,
And here escape
From all that was to all,
Lost beyond loss.
So in the air I toss
Remembrance and rememberer all confused
In a light fume, the last power used,
The last form found,
And child and woman and flower
Invisibly fall through the air on the living ground.

5

I have stood and watched where many have stood
And seen the calamities of an age
Where good seemed evil and evil good
And half the world ran mad to wage
War with an eager heart for the wrong,
War with a bitter heart for the right,
And many, many killed in the fight.

In those days was heard a song:
Blessing upon this time and place,
Blessing upon the disfigured face
And on the cracked and withered tongue
That mouthing a blessing cannot bless,
Blessing upon our helplessness
That, wild for prophecy, is dumb.
Without the blessing cannot the kingdom come.

6

They walk high in their mountainland in light
On winding roads by many a grassy mound
And paths that wander for their own delight.

There they like planets pace their tranquil round
That has no end, whose end is everywhere,
And tread as to a music underground,

An ever-winding and unwinding air
That moves their feet though they in silence go,
For music's self itself has buried there,

And all its tongues in silence overflow
That movement only should be melody.
This is the other road, not that we know.

This is the place of peace, content to be.
All we have seen it; while we look we are
There truly, and even now in memory,

Here on this road, following a falling star.

7

Yet in this journey back
If I should reach the end, if end there was
Before the ever-running roads began
And race and track and runner all were there
Suddenly, always, the great revolving way
Deep in its trance; – if there was ever a place
Where one might say, 'Here is the starting-point,'
And yet not say it, or say it as in a dream,
In idle speculation, imagination,
Reclined at ease, dreaming a life, a way,
And then awaken in the hurtling track,
The great race in full swing far from the start,
No memory of beginning, sign of the end,
And I the dreamer there, a frenzied runner; –
If I should reach that place, how could I come
To where I am but by that deafening road,
Life-wide, world-wide, by which all come to all,
The strong with the weak, the swift with the stationary,
For mountain and man, hunter and quarry there
In tarrying do not tarry, nor hastening hasten,
But all with no division strongly come
For ever to their steady mark, the moment,
And the tumultuous world slips softly home
To its perpetual end and flawless bourne.
How could we be if all were not in all?
Borne hither on all and carried hence with all,
We and the world and that unending thought
Which has elsewhere its end and is for us
Begotten in a dream deep in this dream
Beyond the place of getting and of spending.
There's no prize in this race; the prize is elsewhere,
Here only to be run for. There's no harvest,
Though all around the fields are white with harvest.

There is our journey's ground; we pass unseeing.
But we have watched against the evening sky,
Tranquil and bright, the golden harvester.

The Toy Horse

See him, the gentle Bible beast,
With lacquered hoofs and curling mane,
His wondering journey from the East
Half done, between the rock and plain,

His little kingdom at his feet
Through which the silver rivulets flow,
For while his hoofs in silence beat
Beside him Eden and Canaan go.

The great leaves turn and then are still.
Page after page through deepening day
He steps, and from each morning hill
Beholds his stationary way.

His lifted foot commands the West,
And, lingering, halts the turning sun;
Endless departure, endless rest,
End and beginning here are one.

Dumb wooden idol, you have led
Millions on your calm pilgrimage
Between the living and the dead,
And shine yet in your golden age.

One Foot in Eden

One foot in Eden still, I stand
And look across the other land.
The world's great day is growing late,
Yet strange these fields that we have planted
So long with crops of love and hate.
Time's handiworks by time are haunted,
And nothing now can separate
The corn and tares compactly grown.
The armorial weed in stillness bound
About the stalk; these are our own.
Evil and good stand thick around
In the fields of charity and sin
Where we shall lead our harvest in.

Yet still from Eden springs the root
As clean as on the starting day.
Time takes the foliage and the fruit
And burns the archetypal leaf
To shapes of terror and of grief
Scattered along the winter way.
But famished field and blackened tree
Bear flowers in Eden never known.
Blossoms of grief and charity
Bloom in these darkened fields alone.
What had Eden ever to say
Of hope and faith and pity and love
Until was buried all its day
And memory found its treasure trove?
Strange blessings never in Paradise
Fall from these beclouded skies.

The Incarnate One

The windless northern surge, the sea-gull's scream,
And Calvin's kirk crowning the barren brae.
I think of Giotto the Tuscan shepherd's dream,
Christ, man and creature in their inner day.
How could our race betray
The Image, and the Incarnate One unmake
Who chose this form and fashion for our sake?

The Word made flesh here is made word again,
A word made word in flourish and arrogant crook.
See there King Calvin with his iron pen,
And God three angry letters in a book,
And there the logical hook
On which the Mystery is impaled and bent
Into an ideological instrument.

There's better gospel in man's natural tongue,
And truer sight was theirs outside the Law
Who saw the far side of the Cross among
The archaic peoples in their ancient awe,
In ignorant wonder saw
The wooden cross-tree on the bare hillside,
Not knowing that there a God suffered and died.

The fleshless word, growing, will bring us down,
Pagan and Christian man alike will fall,
The auguries say, the white and black and brown,
The merry and sad, theorist, lover, all
Invisibly will fall:
Abstract calamity, save for those who can
Build their cold empire on the abstract man.

A soft breeze stirs and all my thoughts are blown
Far out to sea and lost. Yet I know well
The bloodless word will battle for its own
Invisibly in brain and nerve and cell.
The generations tell
Their personal tale: the One has far to go
Past the mirages and the murdering snow.

To Franz Kafka

If we, the proximate damned, presumptive blest,
Were called one day to some high consultation
With the authentic ones, the worst and best
Picked from all time, how mean would be our station.
Oh we could never bear the standing shame,
Equivocal ignominy of non-election;
We who will hardly answer to our name,
And on the road direct ignore direction.

But you, dear Franz, sad champion of the drab
And half, would watch the tell-tale shames drift in
(As if they were troves of treasure) not aloof,
But with a famishing passion quick to grab
Meaning, and read on all the leaves of sin
Eternity's secret script, the saving proof.

If I Could Know

If I could truly know that I do know
This, and the foreshower of this show,
Who is myself, for plot and scene are mine,
They say, and the world my sign,
Man, earth and heaven, co-patterned so or so –
If I could know.

If I could swear that I do truly see
The real world, and all itself and free,
Not prisoned in my shallow sight's confine,
Nor mine, but to be mine,
Freely sometime to come and be with me –
If I could see.

If I could tell that I do truly hear
A music, not this tumult in my ear
Of all that cries in the world, confused or fine;
If there were staff and sign
Pitched high above the battle of hope and fear –
If I could hear.

Make me to see and hear that I may know
This journey and the place towards which I go;
For a beginning and an end are mine
Surely, and have their sign
Which I and all in the earth and the heavens show.
Teach me to know.

The Late Wasp

You that through all the dying summer
Came every morning to our breakfast table,
A lonely bachelor mummer,
And fed on the marmalade
So deeply, all your strength was scarcely able
To prise you from the sweet pit you had made, –
You and the earth have now grown older,
And your blue thoroughfares have felt a change;
They have grown colder;
And it is strange
How the familiar avenues of the air
Crumble now, crumble; the good air will not hold,
All cracked and perished with the cold;
And down you dive through nothing and through despair.

An Island Tale

She had endured so long a grief
That from her breast we saw it grow,
Branch, leaf and flower with such a grace
We wondered at the summer place
Which set that harvest there. But oh
The softly, softly yellowing leaf.

She was enclosed in quietness,
Where for lost love her tears were shed.
They stopped, and she was quite alone.
Being so poor, she was our own,
Her lack of all our precious bread.
She had no skill to offer less.

She turned into an island song
And died. They sing her ballad yet,
But all the simple verses tell
Is, Love and grief became her well.
Too well; for how can we forget
Her happy face when she was young?

Impersonal Calamity

Respectable men have witnessed terrible things,
And rich and poor things extraordinary,
These murder-haunted years. Even so, even so,
Respectable men seem still respectable,
The ordinary no less ordinary,
For our inherited features cannot show
More than traditional grief and happiness
That rise from old and worn and simple springs.
How can an eye or brow
Disclose the gutted towns and the millions dead?
They have too slight an artistry.
Between us and the things that change us
A covenant long ago was set
And is prescriptive yet.
A single grief from man or God
Freely will let
Change in and bring a stern relief.
A son or daughter dead
Can bend the back or whiten the head,
Break and remould the heart,
Stiffen the face into a mask of grief.
It is an ancient art.
The impersonal calamities estrange us
From our own selves, send us abroad
In desolate thoughtlessness,
While far behind our hearts know what they know,
Yet cannot feel, nor ever express.

'I Have Been Taught'

I have been taught by dreams and fantasies
Learned from the friendly and the darker phantoms
And got great knowledge and courtesy from the dead
Kinsmen and kinswomen, ancestors and friends
But from two mainly
Who gave me birth.

Have learned and drunk from that unspending good
These founts whose learned windings keep
My feet from straying
To the deadly path

That leads into the sultry labyrinth
Where all is bright and the flare
Consumes and shrivels
The moist fruit.

Have drawn at last from time which takes away
And taking leaves all things in their right place
An image of forever
One and whole.

And now that time grows shorter, I perceive
That Plato's is the truest poetry,
And that these shadows
Are cast by the true.

ADRIAN STOKES

Kouros Statue

We are the light of honey by the death
    That stings us on.
Trauma seals the withering of champions of love
And irreconciliation quickens loving
Nurtured by the anger of its soils
By airless loams from which to rise.
So for our health death must not die,
So breath, smell, phlegm, tactile sweat
Conspire within the syndrome for this shape
    Figured inert by the stone.

While frames of living crumple,
Each flesh inch saunters in its ill obtuse as gut,
    Kouros statue
Promises procession that shall join
The armatures of health from youth to youth;
That this to life from lifeless stone,
Good images upon the plinth
    Amassed from infant times,
May not be numb, hidden in our horror bed
In misery, pollution and the Camp.

Private View

These faces known
Some spoken into
Over forty years.

Thereby ageing them a little more
Paintings look back
Add customary weight
Of new experience.

The clear-cut artist
Or is he here? – it makes no difference –
Speaks more candidly
Than we have done to one another
Whose voices will not cease to grope
Or flourish an impertinence.
We ourselves don't work as valued art.
So each year gaps occur upon the wall of time
Thefts calmly viewed as if by sharp custodians.

Glee Measures Envy

More deeply wanted than of rote
No discourse yet has nailed the gloat
The smooth smug zest, the metalled smile
Though miser's glee has had its note
        And envious Jago;

But not another's loss slows down
    One lap of envy torments' pace;
    A stranger, even, dying first
    Or slips releasing ridicule
    Or culture based on 'face'

Prepared at cost to fend off glee
Lest others should be envy-free
And thereby envied for exempt
Less prone to hate the good as good
    Since triumph is contempt.

Counting

I

Nothing could be numerous without number
    Without the excessive noughts
Through space and time to inconceivable light years
    Or as the thousand millions dead
    And rock that sea, once to their view
    Covers, uncovers, pours away
      Perpetuating foam
To form a speck in mountain piles of one man's thought:
    For us who counted first the fingers of one hand,
    To the unaccountable still slaves;
    Discounted siblings who had narrowed love,
    Alive to mother, home, one day, one tree.

II

    Travelling in multitude,
    Using up the megalithic yards
    For transit of four thousand years
    – A B.C. start, A.D. at the turn –
    Our journey bides the lintels of Stonehenge.
    Some hundred miles provide untold events
    To be compacted into log-like stone.

    If epochs, if a happening were not mapped
    Were Hellas discontinued from our path,
      Back home would be with death.

Suburban Song Thrush

The roof-pipe gurgles:
Woodland is short of liquid for the note
The bird distils
On poured out brick with sad interstices
On built-in sorrow of the chimney stack.

The roof-pipe gurgles
As climate breathes and shifts a load aloud,
The houses gaunt
But for the bird-chant pressing out
To penetrate and sublimate the brick.

At Hythe

I hear from bed at Easter
The drawl – drag pebble's hiss
Breakwaters and steep beach.

It's early light, before footfall.
The damp docile esplanade gives Nature a chance
Arrangement with tenants, Martello tower owners.

I aged seven, warm, barely awake
Night's pebbles cold and glistening and uncountable
The abasement of Nature.
The day's still, the pauses long, the respiration
Delirious.
The sea breathes as if asleep, shifting and sifting
Stickler luminous dreams.

I know Nature as London's hum.
Headland of Folkestone is behind my head, there,
Glowering, aimless.
Behind Sandgate the camp of Shorncliffe.

No one moves, no one counteracts the coiling pebbles.
That or people are on top?
Does Folkestone's ambivalent point
Far from excitement decide its look?

Philip my eldest brother still asleep
Unravels stones with hammer, doesn't chatter.
I might content myself with half his dream.

Today's first horse-tram
Comes uphill to level sea

With mushroom seat at either end
On to the long straight road to Sandgate

By breakwater, by sea's
Chinking piles of lonely stones
That drag on dizzy moments
Breathing hard then lost.

West Penwith

I

The folded hills abolish pace
Break arc where valleys tie.
Spread before a brightening sea
Slow granite farmlands lie.

Outhouses and the hedges' stone
Retrace unmeagre time.
A gleam of sun makes herd the gem
Metallic rock a rhyme.

Approximations gold with beast
Involve a hoard, a heart;
To look on glowing milksop field
Pans nugget life apart.

II

Even tempestuous seas
    Have ease:
In waterfall the torpor
    Of rivulet
Is smoother than the surfaces
    Of rock.

Stone and its runnel are lent
    Our bent;
In active role the passive,
    Of constancy
Our surface to the weather, schemes
    To air.

Recurrence

I

Letter on letter in high top room
Edwardian infants scream their vowels
      In unison.
The siren binds the northern sky
      A coil of morning
A long embodiment of plenitude.

Sixty years, at that same hour, now south
The unhindered sources sound anew
      Identical
Urge on those skies to point and feed . . .
      A pause with letters . . .
A long embodiment of plenitude.

II

Distinctiveness topples as the foam
      When sea envelops mind
Reborn in wave-band hue.
      Wave breaks, encompasses.
Our wits thus shed afresh in spray
      Use impulse to repeat,
Repetitions, psalms
      Tugged on by seamen.

We observe and spy and bathe
      But cannot comprehend
The overspill save *tabula rasa*
      Power in being
Save repetitive bents

The lead to death:
And aching loss brought to the shore
Thunders there across the stretch.

Buildings

I

I hear in spring the sound of iron:
The iron strikes back on day
Swift sparks of certainty
Among the scaffolding
Against a burnished sky.

Less deft, a voice between the blows
Continues with the street
Long settled, mean and tense
Though rungs now share and planks
Our emblematic frame.

II

Gates, quad
Window on to trees.
The afternoon
Won't reach to what
Survives here best
And makes the absent tea
Epitome of want.

Our sight divides world view.
Trees' soughing passes you
Should you then turn about?
Despite our looking through
This window will see us out.

Car Body

Most faces stop an increment for limbs
As car-dismounting now the knees
And soon it's torso
Then peeringly ordaining head appear.

We will have judged the loosened limbs
Until, unless, looks undermine.
Now legs are posts
The veins shall dry.

It's plain as plain could be
That nose affects curved value of the knee
Countenance the foot
Since first and only good and so the bad
– Now quickly scanned upon this dial –
Possessed alternate once the self-same flesh.

Underground Rush Hour

Naturally no talk of fancy medieval beakers.
    A lot of health in lifts
    As figures stand
    Alert with lit-up faces
    Slow hair, the heads unmoved
    By crude crash gates.

    Strangers thus concentrated tight
    Possess no lax recourse
    Nor even watch except the barren shaft
    That soon gives way to open barren street
    To incidents, maybe, of warmth and life
That like oiled runnels keep those foreheads smooth.

With All the Views

The lens is brimming with the crystal view:
Now shoot your rape of natural land
Held far more fast than by familiar ways.
You have it pat: no after-glances please:
Dismiss as wholly captured, I entreat
And learn no merit of my house to cheat,

A slowed-up camera, domicile of glass
   So apt for contemplative exposures;
Though all-purpose mechanism for my living in
Throughout its length invaded by long perfect views
   By panorama and obedient down
As from excrescence observation-post
   Well up a tree.

Our model structure is an occupation force – O.K. –
Wherewith without a nod, we exercise our right of sight;
Strayed, stranger look, but yet more innocent
Than civil styles, bestowed upon a hill,
That sought out formulas to match or dominate a scene.
Yes, if you like, we dandle lands within our ugly knees;
Prehensile power, full tensile play-pen strength
     Open yet inviolate,
Varies each hour exhausted toys: they cannot pall.

While staying here, please make yourself at home . . .
The best of Nature is its nerveless face
Bright, glowering, or the rain
Torn through our massive and unhindered glass
A mirror wall that holds the domus up,
Translates Out into dry, all-spacious In

Where slow identity seems known like unwarped board . . .
    There, there, I want your news:
Your anecdotes imprinted on this varied tapestry of land
Were cut apart by neat, blank margins of our space.

Earliest Memory

Three-hour feed for anger hole:
Coal clatters on the ember mouth
Then cracks the chimney's breadth with silent smoke.
Didn't hot cot soften the traumatic?

In this shocked and shocking place
Grit strangles grit
Frizzles with the blackest thought . . .
Later, clouds of glory gather.

In extremes – so common the extremes –
Innocence, the infancy
Divides with that clean split
Our loss, our sadness, must repair.

Early Wrong

How old the Trojan horse
Armed, boxed with stealth
    Ruler of entries
    Who unseen
Unties the inner hoard.
Though this of him becomes part-lost
    To his main mind
What glee what infant's glee.

Smugness is infantine.
Sly capture mars an outer love
Bites on secret currency
Small coin, large coin.

For glee, confusion of person,
For glee and envy the perdition of the world.

Brief Sermon on Love

Need, great need, gropes in blindness
Past a lightning dream.
Embodiments that hide in flesh
Fulminate when limbs enmesh.

The love beyond the one so large for self
Which hardly grew
But stays, this love that's new
Finds full, uncalculated

A good in way of truth
The ownership another's
To which the dedication brings
Rings encircling other things

Rules out a form of infant mind
Whose loved good thing cannot be heard
Since wired within as captured bird
And kept, this infant pseudo-dove
Smugly controlled, a power preferred.

Then infantile maturity prevails
Model child that's sitting pretty
Under table where the parents sit
Whose choice bits meanwhile seemly howl
Also prisoners in his bowel.

London Childhood

Red meant soldiers, angry flowers.
Ducks, dull colour on the Serpentine
    Pursue or avoid a colloquy
Without surround the child has thought.

Old dry bread was truth those days
Bread floating water-logged and stale;
    First birds snatch all
And well-fed child the crumb.

Amid the hunger, the surfeit
    Of Edwardian age
Starched men were rich in elbows
    Unripe pink. To Elgar honour.

The man-made ties that bind each cult
    Are primitive.
The ducks have since become continuum:
    Each cult swims fast among the rest.

Charles the Martyr

Charles the Martyr
Castrated father I suppose
Huge equestrian portrait by Van Dyck
Our cynosure for latency
Solicited no help, nor gave.

Where was the block
Perhaps by half of one degree
The burning oil that I could mitigate?
But Charles who had not yet been hurt
Repeatedly rode on.

How shout through oil
Long dried it seemed upon this wall?
He was on honeymoon with horse and page
Before the infant's wish had scored
Whereby prime aristo is unrestored.

Street Ignorance

Home streets enwrapped the resolute home vows
    When lifted by a huge Edwardian hat
I had been blown along: and now a search
      – The intersections first –
     For what was deeper meant
  At what was pointed, as if in pointing still,
  As if distance and the suffering thoroughfare
  Could hold the warmth or failure to be mine
  Though unreversing vehicles trample on that time;
    As if the after years were crowds in space,
    Adjoining purlieus earlier unknown.

  There, nothing answers to my time.
  So revisiting the sworn-by streets
    I blunder on the thoughts
    Their pavements won't admit,
  Appalled my dead are laid out as the road
  Or under changeless intersections
  Here where I had changed what others meant
  Where blinds shot up then ceaselessly pulled down
  Today's light signals mechanically relent.

In Cities Once

I

Planted in the London streets
The hollyhocks of horses' hooves
Cluster at the fringe of dreams
Thrusting lifting from the road
When our drill to bud was new.

Burdened by the clanking drays
Though plotted for their servitude
   Under governance of whip
Horses drew green journeys from the mind
   Through landscapes often meadowless:

Perhaps their loud shod rhythms bedded out
   In flower of sparks from touch between
      Road surface and luxuriant being
   Could teach conjunction to each city's school of art
Of roundness sent from belfries when the sound is all.

II

A fallen horse, a splintered shaft
   A visitor collapsed in blinkers.
These streets were once an orchard and a field.

Intact, it seems, and one in flesh
At last Edwardian happening:
A sudden road-based construct silently

Is stranded with the crowd at sea
For whom the street resumption matters.
Now astride the head they change to mobile.

Wintering in Herts

In Hertfordshire the troubled mind:
   The skeletons of plants:
November stillness laps the M1 roar:
   Pine, saddened pine, confronts the Sunday cedar.

Like blue-bottles, like relicts,
In rooms between long passages,
Children, sudden voices,
Divide among themselves a dozen words,

Retrospectively observe their feast
Those wintry few miles away,
The spread of sanity at home
Now crumbs of love and uselessness to faded lawns.

So we knew the most the need for names
The boys', the masters', every noun:
We patched continuously a curtain of the known
   Held as common in expanding light

Then crumpled, bundled for a drawer
When on our knees, on 'let us pray'
Our fingers suddenly clasped darkness . . .
   Let us exorbitate afresh:

'To branching from the bole commit us all:
Teach of your roots the acorn handles soil:
May oak trees foil recurring hurt at night
Resume in mind with all the acorn power.'

In Adolescence

I

Intense bright green in May:
  Unbroken thunderclap:
  Thin leaded sky:
Aching breeze flares on leaves
  Fumbles the livid wood.

Sadness of lush plains:
  Tentacles afar
Of histrionic light withdrawn.
  The bright greens mourn in weeds.
  The birds above revert.

II

Hurrying clouds reveal the coin of moon.
  Certainty portrayed?
I watch sheltered in the prim
  Verandah's basket chair
  Tortured.

The light is plain. I turn
  Return
  Sink into the chair.
The sky moves fast and tranquil
Re-ushers the performer's disk
  Drama with no fixed run
  Uncertain end
Measured in a stumbling sky.

Climacteric

I

Black canal, a summer frock
Iron and bright new grass
   Outskirt of the town
   That afternoon.

Factories in the glance of Sunday bells.
Where rushes showed the bed
   The week just gone and week ahead
   Lolled intertwined.

Light lay on bushes, rushes part:
We left the tow-path for the dizzy field.
   The sedges held out open years
   When we came back.

II

Under slow orchestrated sky
Evening joining this quiet place
   More gradually becomes.

A pond of air enfolds each thing:
   Translucent pearl spreads easiness
To regions of the night.

I watch peaks disengage
Lago Maggiore unmask its depth
A convent front look frank.

   We meet alone
On this great forehead of the hour
That brings you face to face.

Avowal

After hoarse extravagance of light
The evening sips the skies' pure white
From this terrace dome; clarifies our ease
As pour and pound to seas now slowly raucous
    Retrieve your few low consonants
    Or else expand the surge of blood
    In unanimity with waves.

Your words heard so distinct, dear sound,
Hint passages between dark trees,
Between the radiance, tomorrow's dawn.
More than for paths our well-being moves,
Shall move among this hour we know as seas
    Perennial in the days and months,
    One with the blood in all our time.

At Night

Tonight the electric train
On fast lines of noise swaying through a mono-search
   When tentacles of London are thereby swept
   When wind is to the south.

These passing links of sound change to an upright thread
Soar in joints and spokes that square the firmament
As if many heterogeneous towns could make a theme
As if the dying cells of being had better fate.

Such thin such straight progressive forms start stirs of manic
   hope
(Without reference to the millions that lie asleep
Or there jump up)
Hungry and more barren than a dream, lord over space
The room of spaciousness packed close along the wires
A pattern that leans on sound, on what in darkness is not seen.
London is name for conurbation, daylight shows.

   I rest now on the pillow in changed mood
   In crescendo of trains that renew their thread.
A language passes close among them as they run
   A rhythmic beat below the speed.
I turn inward to the quality of sleep
Safe in amicable and coasting parts
   Unbroken pledges that will promise peace.

States of Mind

I

Intent on one-eye lens, on luggage sent ahead
Till death re-photographed with half a view
We lack the broader landscapes in between.
Fun is abstraction, not as we've read.
We judge those times as good which should have been.

The avenues are leafy in the dawn alone.
Painful constructs for ungenerous day
Had narrowed flow of feeling in each home.
No one's trick will solve what's kept at bay,
In rooms of meeting as we inter-roam.

II

Images of love display show cases
And recumbent midfloor of further rooms
Many marbles as if I housed today
A sculpture hall whose guards have gone away.
Shaped by this company I'm with their arms
That shine their satisfaction on a thought.

ADRIAN STOKES

Based on Science

I

In a happening like raindrop
Past, future, every generation
      Will have gone.
Find the feeling in this language.

Accustomed, we were accustomed to death:
Live with lapse of history now, with ease
For a paranoiac and if he fails
For one of millions more.

II

  Sound orchestrates things seen
In a silence we attend their hush.

  The day is still
Woven on moor the moss
And flower bell made to throb
  On anchored stem
  By a grain of air.

A droning bee forms enclave
Is settled and absorbed in quiet.
A word will change the look of things.
Long words annul the world to end.

Italy Once

I

Presiding houses gleam
Flush aperture, smooth wall.
Women wear black, the old
Are mountains of complaint.
Hungry habitually we taste injustice.
Pink houses never wearisome
   Mingle with violence.
   We speak loud;
   Evenly.

II

Olive, vine, stuccoed gateway
Disjoined, agleam upon our hill
   Near to our house
   Communicate the even years
Near our smooth court that seems to lip the sea
Concise, unsloping where the table's laid.

Our panorama signals near approach
Collected far like love.
A sound has sovereign air,
Sea I call enfolding and untaught.
   The land builds from itself
   This separate statuary of trees.

III

Sky plain carafe, wine ruby sound
The hour pours fresh upon our environs.
The passing speaker-van's firm words
Now deep, some purple, brim the far-away,

In trickling steadiness express address.
And wide-flung as we seize the terrace view
White silence sets al fresco of the day.

IV

Blue-throated air and sound
Complexioned by the light
Remark a dome that feeds yet feeds upon
The sky.

Firm citation from a glance
Clear cities, hills and sea
Replenish statuaries of form in me.

Olive trees enact a myriad limit.
Giotto
The careering yells of swallow
House Paduan spring.

V

Seas, olive trees: but leaves
Distinct on terraces of stone
Imbue grey foaming with physique
Construe a branch
That clothes the hill-side rib
As bather in the hour of sun.

Piccolo paese
Each oblong lit
Curves as pendant hung on ridge.
The placid houses look alert:
Gratefully we allow this scene
That their smooth verve has ever been.

VI

Level as whistle through the teeth
In Genoa as the level blue
It pierces through
A consummation note
Of peacock-loving day
Spurts from the engine's throat

Possesses contour stress
Embraces settlement
Steep places of bright tenement
Sun-flash and in sudden shade
The louder boom from port low down
A brink the nerveless sky has made.

Untiringly uncrumbled skies confound
A pilgrim's umber-ridden ground
Absorb elation with the stripe of sound
Pellucid, stare uncloudy as before
Impale unhidden tumult in a home
From dust rebound to lighten Rome.

Rapallo, Kusadasi

Forts, in our time prisons, rock-embedded
That through embrasure soon appropriate
The southern dawn, as if the seas caress:
Rapallo, Kusadasi, head with tongue to land.
Now the light sparks to brilliance.

No prisoners today: the dungeons creamed:
No ferment hidden in the slit-lit cells:
And so the flag is needless and the tower,
Incorrigible crowning by the sun,
The adjuncts of redoubtable address.

Except there now approaches from an all-night fish
    Hard set for land
A boat with one-mind mast still wallowing in night,
Where dying, dead, on dawn-lit boards
Lie prisoners of openness, as yet the headed
    Victims of an endless air.

Horizon's ours, of us who feed on air:
Boat, fort, the nearer shore
All seen alone is our domain
While ferment gathers at an opaque depth
Of unseen being where our lame fetters move
That hold a spate of living to the root.

Home

I

The world is full of home:
An angry face beside me in the tube
Is home. A stench
A loving arm
Earn recognition for the stars at dawn.

Our homestead stocked a mead of pain:
Physique, and even terrors of the sky
A stranger in the dark, wide space
Were in the rooms
That are the base of all.

II

Anguish has returned to base:
  Dawn was undamaged:
  The things I see
– Immortality is theirs –
  Expatiate alone.

The lands are fitted to attentive shape.
We have had no hand in it
  No hand.
Oh so many messages and none.

III

One-note cabbage smells
  Permeate like cats
Lengthening a purlieu
To where the Schubert modulations
  Are changing window view.

Illness, nervous neighbourhoods
　　Squalid and sublime
　　Stand in for deeper pain.
　　Favouring regardless people
　　Schubert's last sonatas reign.

Holiday Morning

A light invisible may haunt a long disgust,
Contrive to foster renunciative complaint
A fretting in the transcendental prams;

Wherefore white shoes for cobbles and small shops
As gulls committed to their urgent yell
Define at last an indecision;
Is newspaper untimely bought
Is weekly needed or the more unsought?

But pausing people post-card struck
Postpone their wider eyes
Wedded though it's well past ten
To overnight surmise
To any content dream-screen size.

A Helpless Sky

Loud gulls have come inland to feed
Against the bosom earth. Half-brown
Impoverished furrows are crowded out
Beneath the swoop of grey, a helpless sky.

That was the day, the years; the mist,
And then intrusive light has scorched the scars
Of darkness as of age, the grades of age,
Or brightens and refreshes crops

That grew, were soon consumed, the ground
Made brown again: again the gulls,
White litter on the fields who pick and choose,
Cry prey, predator and a scene inert.

A Swan

Power in lakes is subject to one swan
A white conveyed from dawn
Black shed from sudden cloud that stored the past.
He pinions water
To multiply yet frame his lonely caste.

Seasons are slowed by losses to the sky
Whose surface lines the lake:
The theft is huge to form this lonely streak,
The arching of abyss
With solid neck, plumes stratified and beak.

The eloquent, the sober-seeming swan
Dumb as the lunar void
Impedes antitheses, forbids a mean:
He Zeus, he Leda there,
Narcissus, sometime, to a winter scene.

November Stillness

I

November stillness fortifies arrest.
The skies repeat the vertical of trees.
The houses sworn to furnish wall and brick
Are wrapt and turned away from aftermath.

Contrary passions cancel, concede
Forgo whispering or silence crying
To intimate a blind on blotting-out . . .
Upright in light our ceasing stands.

I would the ending were an outward turn
Rather than inching into deep in-dream
When death-bed flame consumes the surface sheet
Annuls bed length itself in saucepan heat.

II

Autumn absorbs our sadness with its own.
The princes of the melancholy world
Survey and prove no limit to domain
When foundered thought deliberates on pain
So calm and edgeless.

Each cry of loss has won a figured bass.
The stillness holds the rectitude of song
And sombrely a gentle light remains
To show new riches as a life of stains
The old, the changeless.

Wisdom of Age

I see that eyes are not upon this flesh
   That doesn't speak
   Or speaks of age
   The looseness of the grave.

   Eloquence I see
Does not befit the tongue itself
   For I am eloquent.
Who better talks about the man?

Fleetness is nearer to the foot
   Dexterity to hand
Possessed by limbs themselves whereas
My tongue is of the mind or butcher's shop.

The New Year

I

Hereafter not so hard again:
Just one year's examined pain.
Welcome the Happy New Year.

But years together form a tribe
Some sixty tribesmen now transcribe
The snatched-up toast upon this day.

Drink inflames their hostile wit:
Their mania transcends their skit:
Soon the house will be a clinic.

Let them try the pantry stores:
It's pretty empty now indoors:
The stove is almost seventy:

And loud pronouncement through the house
Where tumbling rafters frighten mouse
Meticulously shall kill us all.

II

Anchored snag, age advanced
Into a nob from the mill-race
Or hoisted by riposte of foam
Yet near old lands to fight for
To gradual banks and flattened loam
The easy running back to home,
Obtains release to neither shore
Continues with the mounted roar
Possesses drowning as before.

Party Value

Grip now, swing by parallel bar
That's not much harder to let go:
In small rooms too the voice must rise
Deaf dumb-bell of this exercise.

How would our conference in space
Social but ex-gymnasium be
Removed from spars with side remarks
– Drink's irreversible held glass

Has landed several light punches
On the brain – how would we proceed?
I have some fear you minimize
Commixture of your roots, the past,

Since naturally I've supposed
Medley of enticing milieus
That party cries, the toppling drink
It seems to me can represent:

But space won't raise the quick-read signs
For infant figure and your home
Whereas sipped drink's confusing rim
Flings thoughts as if a pile were trim.

Schizophrenic Girl

Beautiful unbending daughter
   Soft stutter of automation
   Lost in things without
   Oblivious to things as such
Without boundary where boundary should confine
   Giggling, infinitely sad
   Noble in look, gentle
Hugging yourself to preserve a skin
   That barely separates barely resists the air;
Stiff-jointed, bent, muscle-stretched
Day and night against unintegration:
The bond with you has been for sixteen years
   And would that we were free to talk.
A part of you is sane, a part of each of us
   Psychotic
Would that I could commend to you your courage
That I could mitigate by one moment
   Your unhappiness
   Your fear to make us mad
Would that you often spoke unspoken to
Stepped out of active orbit of confusion
By which you keep at bay the horror
   Of your nothingness,
Released muscles of constraint
   The only force you have.
My constant wish is reflex.
You have no inner shut-off space
   You at the centre;
A sack of potatoes instead
Speckled with tears and holes.
This too is living

This too exhausts the years
In problems of the first
   And greatest magnitude.

The Worst

The parted breast returned to take the toll
– That smashed infant trembles: she's uncouth –
The spite sent out tore back to pierce the hole
The hole we call the mouth where all was one.

And common history won't be kept apart
A history of the palace by the schizophrene
The lacking front, stiff scaffolding, taut art
Of secret closet and collapsing scene.

The stride is wide, her forward body tense
Though still half-shaken by a giggling teat:
Basins vibrate near pins of wizened sense . . .
Salute our Giacometti, and salute the street.

First Lesson

I

Though parents monolithic in their good and bad
Be unhewn structures eternalized within
    First lesson for the young,
    Unevenness of man
Maimed, unmarried parts, undeveloped limbs
    Even some psychotic patches.

A finding out is naive:
See each surprise is small:
Retrace mosaic and unfinished wall.

II

    Expletives boast of stuff unqualified
    Opposing any epithet:
    Meanwhile all other substances procure
    Varied adjectival judgements
    The often sudden prisons of our love.
    Each good thing refers to life entire,
    To absolutes, the filth and death.
    However exquisite the tyrant's rage
    Her waste his purchase with the paramour.

Good Objects

I

The best mind owns an elemental need
(It could be Eliot, at last)
Of other body images
Perfecting satisfactions of their love
(It could be hierarchies, the past):
Protector of their goodness with his own.
The honours, well achieved, to them,
To them, the happiness.
These, the Elysian steersmen, can use
Lifeboat rescue or a summer cruise.

II

Over from the house
Near the traffic's nervous edge
The ripples of the opus Bach
Contained, continuous, for ever.

At once I am as I would be
The house of implemented fugue
Prolifically sane.

A bird sings in winter:
Inner music has no blame,
Marches with the outer sphere.

Some press: the hyacinth can't be pressed
To out-do pus. All, all, the wintry lane,
The complicated way to where
The treasured dear may reign.

III

Day's bad visitor stays all night.
    Mind frequents the look and person.
How forget your face, we know the urge,
    How could love be strange?
    Every infant is most haunted.
I hold an image manifold, a touch
Upon others, tinges sky, spreads in sleep.
    I have no tune, no judgement
    Without the colouring upon them.

Visitant

At once we clasp the bird diagonal
That marks the sky on our attentive being.
We watched the slanting through the square of air
Until a screen, the trees, translated you
      To images enthroned
    Corporeal in space, in
  Landscapes gladdened by your line.

Your wings of chequered settlement remain
As flutterings imprint across the mind
With all of distance folded into fibre
The open contour from beneath your peak.
      You offer us the hills:
    Journeys homeward shine your eyes:
   Valleys lurk upon your breast.

Recall

No sound to window-sill itself
   Nor volume ruling sky;
Each thing absence of all other things
   Condemned a differing tie.

Thought and fear of absence pressed
Throughout this shrunken room
Distraining on an emptied wall
Substantive in gloom.

So I hang your image there
Now points cadaver;
A thing as thing alone
Must lack its flavour.

Meaning of manifold has drained
From poem to common way
But all death's racial purity
Makes mongrel of dismay.

Soft dove in being here
Release the bond with death;
Raise hyacinth from winter's clamp
Leave Merioneth.

In Summer

I

Horizons are near
My arm embraces
Building and shining trees.
Sky is awning. You
Notify reliant air . . .

Silence retreats with you away:
Silence and empty hours were new
Until the void was robbed of fashioned space
When avid loss came crowding into view.

II

The unhappy speak of happiness like this;
It's not so sudden but a long sane plane, a sum
Wherewith the pattern sense may solder gap with Mum
And chimes will often mime aloft the love of people;
Even moving traffic has its steeple
Yet you suffer less elation:
We see felicity as re-formation.

From Memory to Physical Pain

I

Name, name, the owner dead
  Teodolinda,
Old sound without a head
And sadness in a name renewed,
In panoramas that enclose a deed,
In elm a name beyond your tree.

II

Even death pain ignores
But for death's perfect ignorance
  Of pain:
Pain else that has no words
Of resonant calamity
Is ignorant of all
Withdrawn in memory
Fulsome memory, from acute recall.

Metropolis

T.V. ah the rallying voice
But every day more deeply known
Mad volley from a lorry bursts.
The serial events we meet in street
Pick out a silent thought.
The pipes beneath subjoin no bond.

This harsh placenta hatefully
Exaggerates our state;
A town exaggerates our being
From parents' private enterprise
Under Authorities' ukase
Their joining Corporation maze.

The city it is you and I
Scarcely community nor represents.
Great cities are themselves unknown.
With this new model each alone
Employs his sober tone
Naming municipal network.

Out of London

Country seizes out from mind
Participation, distant trees,
Restores to half-remembered shapes
Their intervals
That under long London sway
Were powdered into glints
The many forms conterminous
Exiled beyond the eyes
Emptied between the brows
And hills were unattainable
Like roofs.
Instead of louring space
The rush of streams survived
Or fields that stemmed from stiles.
Cows calling lacked slow jaws.
The farmhouse had intent
Without presence with a doubtful sky.

Now air has regained touch
Ambiguous, and much
For which no framing in the mind can serve.
There's room for lies
They hide in grass
The comprehensive green.
Unfurled spasmodic sky
Is afterthought of things
That were not said.

On Holiday

I

Cars drive far
Through somewhat lordly summer hours
Microbes in the blood of land.

Switched not once
Lamps were lit throughout the past
When by-lanes met the grip of thought.

Travellers
Gain evening for the roadway stop
When with the world the sky expands.

Roads but crest
Near to the rose the Motel sports.
We all pulled up can look at it.

Thing, own growth,
Ourselves, both in and out the car
Abreast of other drivers too.

II

Cloud a steep hummock:
Crowds watch an aptitude of white on green:
Light tunnels into winter:
Days on the wind repeat their names.

Seasons can promise, for a space they lie.
The days will turn afar if left alone.
Inhuman is the human much unknown.
Blindness leads to all our death.

Revenant

A steady cry, unexpectedly supreme
For iron; the cart, the untorn hoof taps
That kick to shape the traffic heap
As if our street might yet aspire to calm
Bring on a vision where an iron includes
The both of want and junk.

The revenant is proof himself
That continuity can thrive.
The horse is fresh, the tumbril whole,
Old iron has use besides the guillotine.
But hear the cry three streets along:
It seems the focal invocation of old hat.

One iron was laid alone upon the cart
Rare as a state for which there's no increase,
    No up nor down,
No mental packaging in reams,
Without excessive eye-lid work: it means:
Wanted, unwanted: peace by this, a single form.